C000252770

DRIVES

BY THE SAME AUTHOR

These Days

DRIVES

Leontia Flynn

CAPE POETRY

Published by Jonathan Cape 2008

4 6 8 10 9 7 5 3

Copyright © Leontia Flynn 2008

Leontia Flynn has asserted her right under the Copyright, Designs
and Patents Act 1988 to be identified as the author of this work

This book is sold subject to the condition that it shall not,
by way of trade or otherwise, be lent, resold, hired out, or otherwise
circulated without the publisher's prior consent in any form of binding or
cover other than that in which it is published and without a
similar condition, including this condition, being imposed
on the subsequent purchaser

First published in Great Britain in 2008 by
Jonathan Cape
Random House, 20 Vauxhall Bridge Road, London SW1V 2SA

www.rbooks.co.uk

Addresses for companies within the Random House Group Limited can be found
at: www.randomhouse.co.uk/offices.htm

The Random House Group Limited Reg. No. 954009

A CIP catalogue record for this book is available from the British Library

ISBN 9780224085175

The Random House Group Limited supports The Forest Stewardship
Council (FSC), the leading international forest certification organisation. All our
titles that are printed on Greenpeace approved FSC certified paper carry the FSC
logo. Our paper procurement policy can be found at
www.rbooks.co.uk/environment

Mixed Sources
Product group from well-managed
forests and other controlled sources
www.fsc.org Cert no. TT-COC-2139
© 1996 Forest Stewardship Council
FSC

Typeset by Palimpsest Book Production Limited, Grangemouth, Stirlingshire
Printed and bound in Great Britain by
the MPG Books Group

for my parents

Oh, tourist,
is this how this country is going to answer you

and your immodest demands for a different world,
and a better life, and complete comprehension
of both at last . . .

'Arrival at Santos', Elizabeth Bishop

Freud had an interesting theory, the Oedipal theory.
You know that all men, he said, want to sleep with
their moms. I thought that was bullshit, until one day
I saw a picture of Freud's mom . . .

Bill Hicks

CONTENTS

ACKNOWLEDGEMENTS

Acknowledgements are due to the editors of the following:

Agni, An Sionnach, Blue Nose, Edinburgh Review, Magnetic North: the Emerging Poets, New Welsh Review, Poetry Ireland, Poetry London, The Times Literary Supplement, The Ulster Tatler, The Yellow Nib

The author is grateful to the Arts Council of Northern Ireland for an award under the Support for Individual Artists Programme 2004, the Ireland Fund and the Princess Grace Irish Library in Monaco.

'Robert Lowell' incorporates a phrase from his poem 'Skunk Hour'. 'Dorothy Parker' begins with the line with which her poem 'Resumé' ends and 'F. Scott Fitzgerald' begins with the opening line of his essay 'The Crack Up'. 'Belfast' contains a line from 'Belfast' by Louis MacNeice. Elsewhere borrowings by other writers are indicated or paraphrased.

SONG

In the silver-grey
dark of your room
your hands are still
nothing is moving

the blinds are drawn
but over and over
the stars rush forward
on your screen-saver.

BELFAST

The sky is a washed-out theatre backcloth
behind new façades on old baths and gasworks;
downtown, under the green sails of their scaffolding,
a dozen buildings' tops steer over the skyline.

Belfast is finished and Belfast is under construction.
What was mixed grills and whiskeys (cultureless, graceless,
    leisureless)
is now concerts and walking tours (Friendly! Dynamic!
    Various!).
A tourist pamphlet contains an artist's impression

of arcades, mock-colonnades, church-spires and tapas bars;
are these *harsh attempts at buyable beauty*?
There are 27 McDonalds, you tell me, in Northern Ireland
('but what are we supposed to *do* with this information?').

A match at Windsor Park has fallen in Gay Pride week.
At two a.m. the street erupts in noise.
I listen as 'We are the Billy Boys'
gets mixed up, four doors down, with 'Crazy' by Patsy
    Cline.

And gathering in the city's handful of bars,
not sunk in darkness or swathed in beige leatherette
men are talking of Walter Benjamin, and about 'Grand
    Narratives'
which they always seek to 'fracture' and 'interrogate'.

DHILLON SEES THE OCEAN:
THE ODYSSEY

Dhillon is travelling by freight train from Minnesota.
Leukaemia stirs in the small bones of his body
– a flurry of poisoned cells, like salt sneaked into tea –
as he sits among loose straw by the yawning doorway
and prairie after prairie scrolls past the wagon.

Laura and Albert Ingalls have joined Dhillon on his odyssey.
Mr Ingalls intercepts them, but elects not to prevent
Dhillon travelling by freight train to San Franscisco.
Night times are worst – rough characters from the sidings.
The children eat baked beans, cold, straight from the can.

As Dhillon arrives in the city, the city is holding its breath.
The traffic seems poised on the pavements, the daytime
tensed as a web for the last, magic touch of the story
– when Dhillon, journey over, sees the ocean
and it is everything he hoped that it would be.

'COUNTRY SONGS'

Of all the emailed jokes and online detritus
that ebbed and flowed, in the autumn, between our
   desktops
the best, we agreed, were the parodied country songs –
titles like 'How can I miss you if you won't go away?'
or 'If you won't leave me alone, I'll find someone else who
   will . . .'

They come back to me now, in these small white days of
   summer
and the joke is less funny, the audience reduced;
the theatre sits in silence – my phoney, lonely-heart
   soundtrack:
'When you leave, walk out backward so I'll think you're
   coming in.'
'If the phone doesn't ring, baby you'll know it's me . . .'

PASTORAL

Noting again the CDs stacked alphabetically,
the shelves distressed artfully, the hardwood boards
which have off-set the bright white colour scheme precisely –
the mild Kildare air, through the smart glass, begins to infect
    my moods.
For this is my leisured weekend in the country!
My father squints at an atlas in search of Kentucky
and whistles the opening bars of 'Memory' or 'Roddy
    McCorely'
into his Fairtrade coffee, absent-mindedly
while presently, in the living and dining space, on the settee,
we discuss fertility! We exchange recipes!
And if we should stray to the subject of prices of property
we do this, strictly, in the spirit of self-parody,
or very quietly. Time passes slowly,
calmly the lights come up on this calm Sunday.

CASABLANCA, BACKWARDS

Rick (to Ilsa): Who are you really and what were you before?
What did you do, and what did you think?

A plane is taking off in a bank of fog.
It leaves the grainy sky, the mapped Moroccan sand.
It is four months since I've seen you. In my hand
the video's controls point in the air.
'Who were we really and what were we before?'
These things are turning over in my mind

as the plane starts banking down. It comes to land
on a grainy fog bank on a concrete plain.
Casablanca backwards; in this version
Rick Blaine sticks his neck out – really – for no one.
As time does not go by; as history gives way to love;
all the rain of Morocco is raining back to the source!
The rain-soaked note resolving into words.
One tear streams back up Ingrid Bergman's face.

VIRGINIA WOOLF

'Why have the body and illness not taken their place
with battle and love as the primary themes of literature?'
Virginia Woolf sits back to admire her phrasing
when just at that moment, an aura – bright, seductive –
starts in one eye. Then voices are heard in the offing.
She leaps from the chair; she is thinking of Lear on the heath.

She is thinking of women in Bedlam, raving, forgotten.
Voices are rising. The tide goes over her head.
As she casts around the desk for some kind of anchor
she is calmed by the solid round of her paperweight.

LEAVING BELFAST

for John Duncan

The planes fly so low over the houses in the east
their undercarriages seem like the stomachs of giant birds;
the skyline in town is the ragged, monitored heartbeat
of a difficult patient; the river holds its own,
and for every torn-up billboard and sick-eating pigeon
and execrable litter-blown street round Atlantic Avenue
there's some scrap of hope in the young, in the good looks
    of women,
in the leafiness of the smart zones, in the aerobatics of
    starlings.

There are good times and bad times, yes, but now you are
burning your bridges, and you are leaving Belfast
to its own devices: it will rise or fall,
it will bury its past, it will paper over the cracks
with car parks and luxury flats, it will make itself new –
    or perhaps
become the place it seemed before you lived here.

HOWARD HUGHES

Glancing down at his patch of North Woodside Road,
Howard Hughes lets the blind fall – then he fixes another
  Mojito.
He's been raving by phone at Hollywood researchers
about 'what I *don't* now about aircraft . . . this is nothing to do
  with my mother!'
The lights in his head are a ring-road filled with traffic,
circling a city, viewed from a plane in the dusk.

'What I don't know about airborne . . .' He flicks a prehensile
  toe
at a greying letter dropped on the rancid carpet.
It's a letter he'll never open – ironically it contains
these words which I never wrote: 'I love you. I'm coming
  home.'

PERSONALITY

'Poetry', you are saying, 'is nothing but personality . . .'
and I look out onto the row upon row of grey hills
and light striking the rooftops, and just at this moment
there isn't much in my life I'd miss if it were over:
the weird cheerful meanness of people to each other,
about pay, status, odd grudges, responsibility;
work's meaninglessness – but its opposite, leisure's abyss!
a snake coiled in the chest morning after morning . . .

How do I cope when poetry is part of this bullshit?
Part of this racket? What you call 'personality'
seems something heroic; it seems the rictus grin
on a student's practice corpse – that breathes iambically
between each line, with their knives parting the skin,
'love me, love me, love me, love me, love me . . .'

SAMUEL BECKETT

'Samuel Beckett suffers from, or has suffered
from: boils, odd facial rashes, phantom pains in his limbs,
nightsweats, insomnia, dreams of suffocation,
palpitations, panic attacks, diarrhoea, aching gums . . .'

His psychoanalyst, Bion, looks up at this point from his
    notebook
and out at the London rain – it is raining on all mankind –
then adds that 'a finger is pointed at Beckett's mother'.
Though, perhaps, of course, it was *nothing* to do with his
    mother.

'It is inconceivable this is not to do with my mother,'
thinks Samuel Beckett. He lopes the long mile to his flat.
He gives a quick shrug at the thought of his last anal cyst.

He returns to his work on *Murphy*, and to reading René
    Descartes:
Descartes whose 'two separate kingdoms', body and mind
(two *utterly* separate kingdoms), *Murphy* later restates.

OLIVE SCHREINER

Olive Schreiner, survivor of four infant siblings,
works just a handful of days in the Royal Infirmary;
she fumbles a test tube, career going nowhere *fast*
as Edinburgh sparkles outside: great buildings and radical politics!
She will suffer from asthma, from 'asthma of the stomach',
from heart trouble, wanderlust, bouts of the blues for decades;
'Oh it isn't my chest, it isn't my legs, it's my*self*,'
she will write in distress to 'sexologist' Havelock Ellis.

Meaning? God doesn't exist – and Olive Schreiner:
author, progressive, free-thinker, feminist,
will burn, like a fuse, from one end of her life to the other.
Her sister is dead, dead too her one-day-old daughter
(her hands quake with passion) . . .

the flame is lit, then extinguished.

SKY BOATS

after Medbh McGuckian (sort of)

An aeroplane caught in the branches of a tree,
struggling over North Belfast's Waterworks,
makes for the open water of the sky.
There is white foam following in this aeroplane's wake

as white plumes follow the yachts across the bay
at Nice and Cannes – and break for an horizon
so indistinct (so blue the sky and sea)
today, we say, the world is upside-down . . .

MONACO

... three weeks now of dull unseasonable weather
here in Monaco Ville. The Cote d'Azur
is not so azure: grey seas, grey skies, grey days ...
'je pense j'ai apporté les temps Irlandais'
I mutter ineptly – as all across the Old Town
spirits get lower as the flags come down
for the Pope, for the Prince; black penitents in procession
have been followed by black memorials placed in windows.
I am making my way amid black-clad security
past a row of black Ferraris at the casinos ...

(March 2005)

BEAUSOLEIL

The sign in your hotel room reads 'ne pas déranger'.
It is too late for that, you think. No discreet
borderline marks this minuscule French town
with its trimmed trees, tasses de café and tabacs,
(which is less a town; which is more a few roads stacked
on the suicide skid from a cliff to the silent sea . . .)
from Monte Carlo, further down the track.
Look, a lap-dog yaps at another lap-dog in the street.

BARCELONA

In Barcelona on the Epiphany
the wise men sail with gifts into the bay.
Two weeks ago it was my thirtieth birthday.
The blue sea glints. Imagine being *thirty* . . . ?
The sculpted seafront stretches out its arms
and gathers up the flashy blue-gold weather.
There are yachts here called *Loti-Lilou, Ginger, Sandrina.*
The city's a glittering slagheap in the sun;
a forest of upright masts, the deserted marina.

ROME

Rome wasn't built in a day. 'Rome?
We will take the lot in one short afternoon.'
Rome! I would like this postcard of the Pantheon
(in Rome!), and also this magnet of the Colosseum.

. . . I can not find Rome. There is too much *Rome* in Rome.
Where's Catullus busting balls inside the forum?
Where's my Roman child in the stone-white hands of Rome:
St Leontia's remnants, robbed from her catacomb . . .

THE LITTLE MERMAID

Spare a thought for this statue, the little mermaid,
suffering, a frozen saint, on the city shoreline.
A baffled crowd musters and ebbs at her elbow.
This is the worst tourist attraction, not just in Copenhagen,
but maybe *anywhere*. O Hans Christian Andersen
your little mer-princesses hung like fruit
out in the boundless wasteland of a cornflower ocean,
eyeballing keels of ships, an iceberg's chassis!
. . . I catch a late flight with Imagination . . .
something is rippling the surface . . . a camera flashes . . .

You can not take one more pace. Each step brings pain . . .

THE HUMAN FISH

We touch down late and meet a long day's heat.
Another budget destination: drain smells,
overarching skies . . . Next day we'll gravitate
to church-cool alleyways instead, to thick-walled stairwells,
or gather, like cows, at water (look a pool
of water leaking from a rusted pipe
gathered into a basin!). The way we keep our cool,
we might be this native beast – this Proteus Anguinus
that fled from the sunlight as from a live volcano,
to be left in the dark: wet, colourless and eyeless
in the caves which they say inspired Dante's *Inferno*.

PARIS

As students march once more on Paris streets
leisured and Euro-ed, we are skilled voyeurs
of the ancient capital's artistic feast.
Chaotic traffic . . . roofs like waterfalls . . .
the same air breathed by Proust and Baudelaire

and Beckett and Stein, Joyce and Apollinaire;
we'll feast upon them in the cemetery –
Jim Morrison and Wilde – look! – oeuvre to oeuvre.
Lovely. Let's metro to Île de la Cité
then join that great big queue outside the Louvre.

BERLIN

Visting Kreuzberg, between Turkish bars
near where the guide says Peter Fechter fell
The Exiles Club and hotspots of the West
where deadbeats boozed and binged – and Bowie *et al*
recorded music so close to the East
the red guards who surveyed them on patrol
should have got writing credits. Here where the past
recent and awful, brick and bullet-hole
stands on street corners – here, the Berlin Wall
reminds you, you say, of peace walls in Belfast.

BOXES

A grey-clad official at a customs desk
– by the outbound flights, or in some border town –
bends on your passport like a feeding bird
on the worm of your struggling . . . indigestible name.

A sudden light comes on in his eagle eye.
He hauls out reams of white, official forms,
a set of bathroom scales, a measuring tape,
a fingerprint kit, a pot of black ballpoint pens.

There are boxes to tick for your name, age, destination,
fields to be filled for your income! The length of your instep!
And the usual cries of 'nothing to declare',
on the part of the detained – tired and indignant.
You write 'Yes Please' for sex?; and 'Northern Irish' – 'N. I.'
Which also, privately, stands for 'N[ot] I[nterested] . . .'

POEM FOR CHRISTMAS

Christmas has come, like cholera, to town.
Women are struggling in the overheated aisles
listening as a piece of music twists like tinsel
towards its end, spools round, then starts again.

At a cue the bars disgorge staff Christmas diners,
who turn to the wall, and, as one man, start to piss,
then move on to other bars, get confidential
on the subject of lost lives, John Peel, George Best . . .

Their toppled glass is the right toast for this city.
To this place of gangsters, double deals and crime rings
I must belong: both of us like to drive
if they can love us, men off one by one
with broken promises. Then *pause* – and seem to thrive
as words and buzzwords rush to fill the vacuum.

(December 2005)

JOE AND ÚNA'S BOAT

We are sitting on the deck
of your moored three-bedroom boat
watching the planes criss-cross
over Canary Wharf

with its great cranes, like darts
in the sky's continuum
that stitch you to the ghost
of the ghost of your home town.

POEM FOR NEW YEAR

Snow covers London, snow covers Glasgow,
snow lies along the West Highland line.
The sap in the trees is frozen
and it makes no sound.

The sap in the trees is frozen
and it makes no sound.
Word reaches us: a friend of a friend is dead
by her own fair hand.

MARCEL PROUST

The blue and gold of a pre-war Indian summer
is not stretched out, like a tea guest, by the window. My
   maman,
perfumed, far-sighted, disciplined, in blue,
is not a point of light passing through each room
on which turns fear and melancholic asthma. Life is a
   sickroom
– a morgue requiring three coats and a muffler.
I have not weakened. I have not lain till noon,
I was not stricken by Samuel Beckett's cigar . . .

But one whiff of kiwi-fruit lip-balm from Anita Roddick's
   Body Shop
and wham! I'm back in the midst of the storm and stress
of over a decade ago. I'm bewildered! Bewitched!
anhedonia's bone-cold hand clutching my throat
like a mugger – in the toils of the bed, believing I'm Marcel
   Proust
giving birth to the bright-white labour of life lived . . .

CHARLES BAUDELAIRE'S MOTHER

This life of vice, depravity and pain
where childhood's a remote, uncanny garden
with intermittent sunshine only (rain
lashing the flowers flat most days), where boozing,
pills and addictions, illness, fucking whores
occupy us thereafter to the tomb
(preferable, mind, to being *fucking bored*)
may be the sick construction of a womb

(for what else drags us here?). Yet nonetheless
to whom, his number up, did Baudelaire
– knackered by opium, racked with syphilis –
turn, we note, but back to his own mother?
'Though meant for gentle love', he writes to her
'I think that one of us will kill the other.'

LA

Freak winds are playing havoc in LA.
The day after we arrive, a billboard sign
propped above Wilshire Boulevard blows down,
and brush fires sweep the slopes of Beverly Hills
– where Frances Ring lives. Frances Ring recalls
the studio system: factory-line and strikes
when simple two-lane roads ran through the valley,
and west-migrating, highbrow lefty hacks,
trying their hands at screenplays, filled the town
with more stars than in heaven. Here, today,
we watch as huge cars snake the boulevards.
A pall of pale blue hangs above the freeway.

WASHINGTON

I met a traveller, walking in the mall
in Washington, in April, *from an antique land*,
map-less, in rapid tourist mode, between
Who said the Washington Memorial
and . . . Jesus fucking Christ . . . this mausoleum
where Lincoln sits in state, and there in stone
fluent and just his Gettysburg address.
Boundless on either side, are wreaths to war.
Look on my works ye mighty and despair.
And by the White House, men with walkie-talkies.

NEW YORK

There are several things we did not want to find in New York:
not the snow which fell this year on the Easter Parade,
not the Calypso phase of Talking Heads' David Byrne,
not the figurative work of de Kooning and Jackson Pollock.
Not the vapour trails which ribbon the city's sky,
not the queue for the iPhone™ outside the Apple Shop,
not no smoke in the bars, not no *real* New York Poets' school,
not the places that are gone from the re-drawn map.

DOROTHY PARKER

You might as well live. You might as well live
in a hotel room downtown
with a dog and a bottle of bathtub hooch – forgive
the world-weary resignation.

You might as well love. You might as well love,
then not, a series of guys – and, of these, marry
a lush first and then a screen-actor of
a kind, who's half fairy.

My mother died when I was five.
My father got religion.
My true lover, death, is a jerk – so I'm alive
in old age and anticipation.
And if you think these words just some glib epigram,
well, I say, make of them what you make of them.

F. SCOTT FITZGERALD

'Of course all life is a process of breaking down.'
You can live it up for as much as a generation
but as sure as the high of economic boom
bursts like a bubble, ushering in DEPRESSION,
as sure as the shiny coin of happiness
(oh, ecstasy to me!) is spent at last . . .
Fitzgerald shifts in bed. He has come west;
his bedside locker slowly fills with empties.

As sure as you get the girl and then get pissed;
as sure as you buy the most impressive car
then drive it off the road . . .
                                    Out of the past
the long trains of our youth come snaking – far
off through the wheat fields . . .
                                    What we were straining for,
Fitzgerald pauses, it was *already* lost.

ALFRED HITCHCOCK

Alfred Hitchcock is watching an ice-white blonde,
groomed to perfection, gunning a neat roadster
over a coastal path. The small waves peak
and ebb away. Who wouldn't want to watch her
slip down a gear to complete a quick manoeuvre,
impassive under her hero's scrutiny?
Hang on, does she not look a little like his mother . . . ?
No. This is a case of mistaken identity.

Hitchcock himself will never learn to drive
on account of his lifelong, much-debated fear
that a copper might pull him over – and give
no warning or reason, but march him from the car

and lock him away in the dark where his terrified cries,
unheard or unheeded, are the cries of a blubbery child.

ELIZABETH BISHOP

Darkness is falling on Worcester, Massachusetts.
Shadows lengthen. The sun slinks past the rooftop
and drops out of sight. Elizabeth has bronchitis.
And asthma. And eczema.
                              'Kidnapped'
from safety, the door which she heard slam
(her mother won't return from the institution)
slams for her too. She thinks it says her name:
orphan, depressive, drinker, lesbian –

and soon-to-be veteran loser. Losing
in many attractive locations: Maine,
New York, and (scene of her near-death
brush with a cashew) Brazil . . .
lost parents, houses: she'll lose exceptionally well,
lover by lover. She even loses her breath.

AIRPORTS

Airports are their own peculiar weather.
Their lucid hallways ring like swimming pools.
From each sealed lounge, a pale nostalgic sky
burns up its gases over far-flung zones,
and the planes, like a child's mobile, hang at random.

Like hospitals, they are their own dominion.
We have tried their dishes with plastic knives.
We have packed our bags ourselves, no one has tampered
    with them,
and as we pass through the eye of the charged needle,
our keys and wallets drop from us like stones.

But now we are passing quicker, colder, clearer,
from East to West un-policed, a gate of light
which lengthens like some animal proboscis
(where has the night gone? what's all this time on our hands?)
or a hoop bowled along at speed beside the sun.
And when we return, the airports remain in us.
We rock, dry-eyed, and we are not at home.

ROBERT LOWELL

I

The milky light of a lobster town in Maine
is light thrown by water. Bleak light. Robert Lowell
in middle age is frizzled stale and sane
he feels his ill-spirit sob in each blood cell.

Back in his childhood were parental rows
really responsible for this big rebellion
against the line — that twists and tangles now —
of Protestantism, of literary tradition,

against the tide of caste marine-blue blood
and *politics*? This government-made warfare
could, in its turn, hardly seem less mad
than mania's 'magical orange grove in a nightmare':
the murdered boys and their returning shrouds
spurring his hell-bent poet's un-scared stare.

II

But imagine leaving his third and unreal wife
in order to return to his suffering second,
revising and revising
as though they were just lines or matters of form

the living details of a living life?
And imagine using those letters in his sonnets?
Using and re-using
the fact of pain — as though pain were a poem;

or as though (old story)
life and art
were, for this poet, as minutely clocked

as his dramatic final taxi journey
(as his heart
in his body) when both stopped.

SATURDAY IN THE POOL

The boy pauses at the end of the diving-board
then dives: a broad sword
cleaving the water – there is parting! And rejoining!
This is reflected back upon the ceiling
where, flippered, supine
– swimming in the cells
and water-pathways of ourselves –
we watch the gases breed: a fog of chlorine.

The boy pauses at the end of the diving-board
then dives: on board
the liberator, big-eyed airmen watch
as the cargo leaves the hatch:
the missile stabs the air
then impacts – megavolts
and gigawatts, primordial lightning bolts –
in whirlpool ripples: clouds of dust and vapour.

Saturday at the pool. A dozen forms
push. Kick. Breathe. Push. Kick. Breathe. Turn
and bring themselves along the tepid length
and breadth of the translucent element
like frogmen. Bone
and blood. Four dozen limbs
– nurses, teachers, wives, *civilians* –
push. Kick. Breathe. Push. Kick. Breathe. Turn.

Outside our youth is laid about the park.
Planes thread the sky like needles. No attack
presents itself. No dogfight
twists above the level of the trees. A kite
is moored in the sky. It peers,
like the boy on the diving-board, down upon the world

where we have crawled: we are raw-gilled
and live. The blood is banging in my ears.

(in the last line 'live' is the adjective, rhyming with 'five')

DON'T WORRY

Don't worry about the government
or this world of pain
or the flood-water which may come inching
from the swollen river, over distant fields.

My heart is knocking
against the wall of my chest
and my womb is knocking
against the wall of my groin

and black shadows may come inching
round my eyes – but don't worry
about famine or war, here in our world
of love. Okey dokey?

WANTS

Over the acres and spaces and pages and screens
news of what we want comes
to keep us informed. Everything is clean
and efficient. Everything saves time.

There is a new version of a thing –
and I want one.
I want to live each day and love the skin I'm in
I want to lose that holiday half-stone.

And when the winter sky leaches and fades out
in town
above Tile Magic or The Game Zone

I want a bed of snow – bleached, whiter than white:
fine linen
and the sheets turned down.

A HEAD FOR FIGURES

The radio crackles. This is not static, it's *facts*:
my virtual inbox seethes with petitions and sex-aids.
FRENCH KISSING TEENS AT RISK OF MENINGITIS.
'Suicide rates are up forty per cent in a decade'
HATE-CRIME BREAKS RECORDS . . . divorces and fuel
    prices
slalom between my paper's rustling pages.
As I exit a busy store in a brand new complex
I count 61 ingredients in my chicken sandwich.

Of the five simple questions the doctor asks my father
he gets just half one right – a mark of ten per cent!
And where have they gone, the rest of those rustling facts?
They have fallen from his head like cerements.
They have slipped through his fingers,
                    they have slipped from his big kind hands.

GEORGE ORWELL'S DEATH

The lamps are lit at half past five on Jura
as the island sinks into shadowy isolation.
George Orwell here has a vision of the future – a
place as stark. He lights a cigarette, thinking.

In every room a kind of two-way screen
whose language says one thing but means another
controls the people (pap will divert the proles)
and chastened by news of far-off, constant war

each man must drag the cross of his own frame
as Orwell, in hardship and illness, now drags his.
One shouldn't, perhaps, smoke when suffering from TB . . .

His work complete, he'll convalesce in Cranham,
planning more books – *one can't die with books to write!*
thinks Orwell to himself. And then he dies.

CYPRUS AVENUE

Van Morrisson is singing 'Cyprus Avenue'
on the car stereo system
when you turn into Mourneview
car park. The ignition

sparked, we grind the gears
of your dad's hatchback
with the sheathed interiors
and practise at the clutch.

An old song plays on the radio
I am captured in a car seat.
On the points of summer and youth
the whole world pivots.

ANNIE HALL

Dear Karen, life isn't easy
when you're spending all your money
on driving lessons and therapy.
But if it makes you happy

feel free to think of me,
as you walk the parched veldt,
motoring insouciantly.
And keep to yourself that

though I may 'drive like Annie Hall'
– as you say – there are those other
days – on which I still
drive like Annie Hall's brother . . .

SYLVIA PLATH'S SINUS CONDITION

Between the long-limbed, gee-whiz, perfect girl
– wearing her gifts, her string of pure, straight As
like a neat sweater and a string of pearls –
and her deeply buried twin (she *ricochets*);

between this blonde self and the darker one,
who breeds an absent father's awful abscess
and mother-fury far beneath the skin,
lie Sylvia Plath's infected sinuses,

lies the fistula: the channel prone to flood,
whose volt of pain and mad, infectious rush
might prove as sudden

as the thought to drive at high speed off the road;
to tear one's flesh – to push push push
the self-destruct button . . .

'WE USE BRILLIANTINE'

Time rushes towards us with its hospital tray of infinitely varied narcotics, even while it is preparing us for its inevitably fatal operation . . .

Bromide and Epsom salts, scotch and barbiturates.
The Pharmaceutical Companies of the 1950s
don't need to be asked twice. The artist self-sedates
for dizziness and mood-swings – sharp anxieties,
which some call 'causeless'. Valium, morphine
soothing the pangs of phantom heart attacks
and, for the blue spells ('we use brilliantine'):
the prospecting and oil-dark wealth of sex.

For the *male* artist, rather; in the shadows
there is a woman standing, and her fears
bat round the room with awful moth-like wings:

aging, addiction, loneliness and madness.
Kind words, perhaps, would ease their awful beating,
but that connection's cut. Choke back the tears.

MILOŠ

You woke up just before the driver did.
Your cheapo, backpack, night-time ride through Turkey
shouldn't have ended *this* way: on the road
(the bus had turned a corner on its side,
grinding up glass and bones. The driver died.
The girl behind you died . . .), half-scalped and bloody
and left, when you heard of bombs or trauma, since
with a sixth-sense of how soft it is, a body.

And how every day is vivid, urgent, clear
as that bizarre 12 hours in Bratislava
where in, improbably, a white-stone chateau
you made your crazed, trilingual pass at me,
which didn't work, and you never stayed in touch —
is a cup of golden light, an orchard grotto.

FOR THE SUICIDE IN THE TATE MODERN

They said your phone rang, then you took the steps
over to the handrail on the top level
and (looking down, the distance telescopes:
the ground recedes, the spiral of a stairwell,
coils and uncoils), as you were stood there, life
lovely to us, to you must have seemed all
the lousy things that sank you to this height.
They said your phone rang, that you took the call,

then fell, and died. The sympathetic trace
(read 'morbid instinct') falters at this part.
After the vaulting over what comes after?

Yours was the shortest journey through this space,
through its thick crowds and the indifferent art,
beyond their reach, further beyond us, *elsewhere*.

DRIVE

My mother's car is parked in the gravel drive
outside the house. A breeze springs
from the shore, and blows against this traffic sign
standing between the by-road and the main road
where somewhere a cricket ticks like a furious clock.
My mother's car is an estimable motor,

a boxy thing – the car in which my mother,
during a morning's work, will sometimes drive
to Dundrum, Ballykinlar, Seaford, Clough,
'Newcastle', 'Castlewellan', 'Analong'.
They drive along the old road and the new road –
my father, in beside her, reads the signs

as they escape him – for now they are empty signs,
now one name means as little as another;
the roads they drive along are fading roads.
– 'Dromore', 'Banbridge' (my father's going to drive
my mother to distraction). 'In Banbridge town . . .', he sings.
She turns the car round, glancing at the clock

and thinks for a moment, turning back the clock,
of early marriage – love! – under the sign
of youth and youthful fortunes – back, in the spring,
the first *great mystery*, of life together:
my mother's indefatigable drive
keeping them both on the straight and narrow road,

and, as they pass 'Killough' or 'Drumaroad',
she thinks of children – broods a while (cluck cluck),
on their beginnings (this last leg of this drive
leads back to the empty house which she takes as a sign) . . .
how does it work, she thinks, this little motor?
Where are its cogs, and parts and curly oiled springs

that make her now, improbably, the wellspring
of five full persons – out upon life's highroads:
a grown-up son, a gang of grown-up daughters,
prodigal, profligate – with 30 years on their clocks?
She doesn't know, and isn't one to assign
meaning to their ways, their worlds' bewildering drives –

though she tells this offspring she's nearing the end of the road
a clock ticks softly . . . the low pulse of some *drive* . . . ?
My mother watches. She's waiting for a sign . . .

WINTER LIGHT

(In 2004 Ingmar Bergman said he was 'depressed' by his own films and could not watch them any more.)

Jonas Persson is worried about China.
In particular he fears that the atomic bomb
lies in her grasp. Off-screen he strokes a trigger.
The pastor, Tomas, cannot comfort him.

The pastor, Tomas, is worried. Man's existence
is one long round of suffering. (High above
the frozen landscape God responds with silence.)
He derives no solace from his mistress' love.

His mistress, Märta, suffers. Eczema
has touched her feet, her hands and the crown of her head,
as if to say: *This is what living's for.*
She also suffers with her periods.

Then comes the churchyard and the black and white
of headstones half in shadow, touched by winterlight.

OUR FATHERS

for Nicky Carey

Our fathers,
the first gigantic men
of the earth – our teachers –
have, at the end,

become creatures,
almost, of air.
What anchors
them (my father's hair

is thistledown,
his smile the slow
swoop of a distant bird, blown
over his body) to now

and to here?
A radar blip
in the darkness; the last flare
fired at sea; the snap

and pop of a synapse
crossed – closing
its spaces . . . and perhaps
he'll weigh in

– hello! – my father,
tethered,
for a bit, by the
least thing. Talk of the weather

is one; laughter
which follows punchlines,
nods – nudge nudge – a handshake:
these are signs

and our calendar
customs – our days, months, weeks,
these are braille
or a trail

of breadcrumbs –
or rosary beads
in his hands (all thumbs)
by which – yes indeed –

we seek to delay
them, our fathers. The fire
is lit. 'Stay'
we say, 'pull up a chair',

thinking – heh heh – if we can trap
them,
then we can keep
them,

and if we can keep them
– we'll keep them . . . forever!
But my father
my father

my father holds open
the door of himself
and lets his old ghost
pass through

before him
('after you, after you'
he mouths): his guest,
– his old self – stealth

-ily tip
-toeing out (Shhh)
– one finger on his lips –
leaving only the hush

'. . .'
of evening – falling
on the households,
(creaking and settling)

of a generation:
on their thresholds
of pain and love – Amen, Amen –
on the townlands.

On the white fields

SPRING POEM

When, in morning light, I walked to the bridge
– that old skeleton propped on ribs of steel –
I thought of my dead father;
but neither his loss, my pain, or near dispersal
into competing selves which flew past others,
drove me to the edge.

Neither this nor thinking of lost autumn nights,
cool and comforting, like when I was a child
and drew up the bed-sheets;
or even – horror – the early, creeping signs
under the eaves and round the colonnades
of growing things;

no, none of this spurred to spring or swallow dive
over the railing, into the abyss
and there begin again;
as every fall, through meaning and its loss,
lets us begin: as *live* becomes *believe* –
in love, oblivion.

DUNGENESS

When we drove together last year through Dungeness
in your absurd yellow car
and passed the gravel pits, the shack, the power-
station – stark, yet not incongruous in the distance –
I insisted on listening to the soundtrack to *Paris, Texas*.

Here were the cottage and lighthouse. You wanted to cut ties
so came to this coast
away from '*You know* . . .' Now I look behind me
and there is our youth among the shingled waste
that recedes before my eyes like the angel of history.

POEM FOR AN UNBORN CHILD

may you be dull . . .

for Dara Jane Flynn O'Dwyer

A shrimp under glass. One pollywog in the pool
of knick knacks and double helices (etc.) – you're
the catch of the day, the kid with the press pass cadged
to check out what's coming. Canny womb with a view
and God's-eye view of a godless world
all stress, storms and sorties, but armed to the gills with love
against bogeymen, beasties, blood-sucking bats – and
of course other humans. Oh radical innocent.

To 'avoid any danger of suffocation'
I 'keep away from children', men with beards
and weird prescriptions . . . but that's as maybe – you

I would wish to be daunted, steadfast – yes – alert
and to swim (in a style of your choosing) to the heart
of *undull* life, that you are magicked to.